TO THE LIGHT

TO THE LIGHT

A Journey Through Buddhist Asia

SHARON COLLINS

To Mariah and Josh,
Sharon Collins

W. W. NORTON & COMPANY

New York • London

IN MEMORY OF
MARIAN HAMMOND COLLINS

I WOULD PARTICULARLY LIKE TO EXTEND MY THANKS AND APPRECIATION TO AMY KOBLENZER, ROBERT M. OLMSTED, STEPHANIE LIGON OLMSTED, ROBERT SCHAEFER, MATT BIALER FOR THEIR UNWAVERING SUPPORT, ASSISTANCE AND ENCOURAGEMENT DURING THE TIME IT TOOK TO PUT TOGETHER THIS BOOK. AND TO NORTON, MY APPRECIATION FOR THE OPPORTUNITY TO MAKE THIS BOOK HAPPEN.

CONTENTS

There is no wisdom for a man without harmony,

and without harmony there is no contemplation.

Without contemplation there cannot be peace,

and without peace can there be joy?

BHAGAVAD GITA 2.66

From delusion lead me to Truth.

From darkness lead me to Light.

From death lead me to Immortality.

UPANISHADS

Remember the clear light, the pure clear white light from which

everything in the universe comes, to which everything in the

universe returns; the original nature of your own mind.

The natural state of the universe unmanifest.

TIBETAN BOOK OF THE DEAD

Let go into the clear light, trust it, merge with it.

It is your own true nature, it is home.

TIBETAN BOOK OF THE DEAD

The visions you experience exist within your consciousness;

the forms they take are determined by your past attachments,

your past desires, your past fears, your past karma.

These visions have no reality outside your consciousness. . . .

[L]et them pass.

TIBETAN BOOK OF THE DEAD

If you become involved with these visions,

you may wander for a long time confused. . . .

[L]et them pass through your consciousness

like clouds passing through an empty sky.

TIBETAN BOOK OF THE DEAD

These are the two paths that are forever:

the path of light and the path of darkness.

The one leads to the land of never-returning:

the other returns to sorrow.

BHAGAVAD GITA 8.26

Considering the two paths, let the wise man walk

on the path that leads to light.

DHAMMAPADA 20.282

The clouds of Light have, like space, no hindrances;

All that have obstructions are not impeded by them;

There is no one who is not embraced in His Soft Light;

Take refuge in Him who is beyond thought.

SHINRAN'S SONGS TO AMIDA

The Self is the light reflected by all.

He shining, everything shines after him.

The Tree of Eternity has its roots above

And its branches on earth below.

KATHA UPANISHAD

Do not be frightened of the intensely bright clear azure-blue light of the supreme awareness. It is the radiant light of this enlightened being, the awareness of the continuum of reality. Try to feel drawn to it with trust and devotion. . . .

TIBETAN BOOK OF THE DEAD

If on the great journey of life a man cannot find one

who is better or at least as good as himself,

let him joyfully travel alone . . . .

DHAMMAPADA 5.61

[But i]f on the journey of life a man can find a wise and

intelligent friend who is good and self-controlled,

let him go with that traveler;

and in joy and recollection let them overcome the dangers

of the journey.

DHAMMAPADA 23.328

It is by living close to a person that his morality is to be known. Then only after a long time, not after a short period; and only by considering that person, not without consideration; and only by one who is wise, not by a fool.

It is by associating with a person that his clarity is to be known.

It is in adversity that a person's fortitude is to be known.

It is by discussion with a person that his wisdom is to be known, and then only after a long time, not after a short period; and only by considering it, not without consideration, and only by one who is wise, not by a fool.

UDANA 6.2

Those who recognize the existence of suffering, its cause, its remedy and its cessation have fathomed the four noble truths. They will walk in the right path. Right views will be the torch to light their way. Right aspirations will be their guide. Right speech will be their dwelling place on the road. Their gait will be straight, for it is right behavior; right employment will sustain them. Right efforts will be their steps, right thoughts their breath; and right contemplation will give them the peace that follows in their footprints.

THE TEACHINGS OF BUDDHA

Samsara, the transmigration of life, takes place in one's mind.

Let one therefore keep the mind pure,

for what one thinks that he becomes:

this is the mystery of Eternity.

MAITRI UPANISHAD

The world's end can never be reached

By means of traveling,

Yet without reaching the world's end

There is no release from suffering.

Therefore, truly, the world-knower, the wise one,

Gone to the world's end, fulfiller of the spiritual life,

Having known the world's end, at peace,

Longs not for this world or another.

SAMYUTTA NIKAYA

Obey the nature of things

and you will walk freely and undisturbed.

VERSES ON THE FAITH MIND
SENGTSAN

If, with mindfulness' rope,

The elephant of the mind is tethered all around,

Our fears will come to nothing,

Every virtue drop into our hands.

THE WAY OF THE BODHISATTVA

Free everywhere, at odds with none,

And well content with this and that:

Enduring dangers undismayed,

Fare lonely as rhinoceros. . . .

And turn thy back on joys and pains,

Delights and sorrows known of old;

And gaining poise and calm, and cleansed,

Fare lonely as rhinoceros.

SUTTA NIPATA

In days gone by this mind of mine used to stray wherever selfish desire

or lust or pleasure would lead it. Today this mind does not stray and is

under the harmony of control, even as a wild elephant is controlled

by the trainer.

They make delightful the forests where other people could not dwell.

Because they have not the burden of desires,

they have that joy which others find not.

DHAMMAPADA 7.99

The perfume of flowers goes not against the wind,

not even the perfume of sandalwood, of rose-bay, or of jasmine;

but the perfume of virtue travels against the wind

and reaches unto the ends of the world.

DHAMMAPADA 4.54

Thunder and lightning and clouds, these three,

When emerging, emerge from the sky itself.

When dissolving, they dissolve into the sky itself. . . .

Self-awareness, self-illumination, self-liberation, these three,

When arising, arise from the mind itself.

When disappearing, they disappear into the mind itself.

THE STORY OF THE ROCK DEMONESS OF LING-BA

MILAREPA

"What do you think, Rahula; for what purpose is a mirror?"

"For the purpose of reflecting, Lord."

"Similarly, Rahula, whatever action you desire to do, reflect, 'Would this action be conducive to my own harm, or to the harm of others, or to both?' And if, when reflecting, you realize that it would cause harm either to yourself or to others, then such an action you must not perform.

"If on the other hand, when reflecting you realize that such an action will produce happiness, then such an action, you should do again and again, abiding in joy, and training yourself in the meritorious states.

"For whosoever purifies their bodily, verbal and mental actions, does so in exactly the same way: by constantly reflecting."

AMBALATTHIKA EXHORTATION TO RAHULA,
MAJJHIMA NIKAYA NO. 61

Beyond the power of sword and fire, beyond the power of waters and winds,

the Spirit is everlasting, omnipresent, never-changing, never-moving,

ever One.

BHAGAVAD GITA 2.24

There are two kinds of patience: the patience of this world

and the patience which transcends this world.

In the patience of this world, we learn to endure hunger, thirst, heat, cold,

suffering and joy. In the patience which transcends this world we learn to be

steady in belief, wisdom, generosity, compassion and open-mindedness. . . .

We learn to endure insults, beatings, taunting, evil plots against us, greed,

anger and ignorance. We learn to endure the unendurable and to

accomplish the impossible.

UPASAKASHILA SUTRA

In the bonds of works I am free, because in them

I am free from desires. The man who can see this truth,

in his work he finds his freedom.

BHAGAVAD GITA 4.14

He who goes for refuge to Buddha, to Truth

and to those whom he taught,

he goes indeed to a great refuge.

DHAMMAPADA 14.190

If no wind blows, then nothing stirs,

And neither is there merit without perseverance.

THE WAY OF THE BODHISATTVA

Leave all things behind, and come to me for thy salvation.

I will make thee free. . . .

BHAGAVAD GITA 18.66

Hear the essence of thousands of sacred books:

To help others is virtue; to hurt others is sin.

HITOPADESA

When you are in deep darkness, will you not

ask for a lamp?

DHAMMAPADA 11.146

All that I possess and use

Is like the fleeting vision of a dream.

It fades into the realms of memory;

And fading, will be seen no more.

THE WAY OF THE BODHISATTVA

The buddhas and the bodhisattvas both

Possess unclouded vision, seeing everything:

Everything lies open to their gaze,

And likewise I am always in their presence.

THE WAY OF THE BODHISATTVA

[B]e ye lamps unto yourselves, be ye a refuge to yourselves.

Betake yourselves to no external refuge.

Hold fast to the Truth as a lamp.

Hold fast as a refuge to the Truth.

MAHAPARINIBBANA SUTTA

The monk who has the joy of watchfulness and who
looks with fear on thoughtlessness, he goes on his path
like a fire, burning all obstacles both great and small.

DHAMMAPADA 2.31

Then his soul is a lamp whose light is steady,
for it burns in a shelter where no winds come.

BHAGAVAD GITA 6.19

See yourself in others.

Then whom can you hurt?

What harm can you do?

. . . . [Y]our brother is like you.

He wants to be happy.

Never harm him

And when you leave this life

You too will find happiness.

DHAMMAPADA

No one can understand the sounds of a drum without understanding

both drum and drummer; nor the sounds of a conch without

understanding both the conch and its blower. . . .

BRIHADARANYAKA UPANISHAD

Protecting oneself, one protects others;

protecting others, one protects oneself.

SAMYUTTA NIKAYA

What is education? Teacher speaking

To the disciple seated by his side,

Wisdom between, discourse connecting them.

Taittiriya Upanishad

To study the Buddha way is to study oneself. To study oneself is to forget oneself. To forget oneself is to be enlightened by the myriad dharmas. To be enlightened by the myriad dharmas is to bring about the dropping away of body and mind of both oneself and others. The traces of enlightenment come to an end, and this traceless enlightenment is continued endlessly.

SHOBOGENZO GENJOKOAN
DOGEN

If we can stop and be still, the mind will have a chance to be free,

to contemplate its sufferings and let them go.

LOOKING INWARD

K. KHAO-SUAN-LUANG

Restraining yourself

And loving others

Are seeds that bear fruit

In this life and beyond. . . .

Seeds turn into plants that bear fruit.

Motives turn into minds that bear fruit.

Seeds are neither severed from

Nor forever fused with fruits of plants,

Motives neither severed from

Nor forever fused with fruits of minds. . . .

Acts, like contracts,

Are as irrevocable as debts—

. . . Only patient cultivation frees you from their grip.

VERSES FROM THE CENTER

NAGARJUNA

Were there a trace of something,

There would be a trace of emptiness.

Were there no trace of anything,

There would be no trace of emptiness.

Buddhas say emptiness

Is relinquishing opinions.

Believers in emptiness

Are incurable.

. . . . When emptiness is possible,

Everything is possible;

. . . . Deny emptiness and you deny

The origins of suffering.

Verses from the Center

Nagarjuna

And if, like the lotus flower, which grows out of muddy water

but remains untouched by the mud,

they engage in life without cherishing envy or hatred,

and if they live in the world not a life of self but a life of truth,

then surely joy, peace, and bliss will dwell in their minds.

BUDDHACARITA

Regard your body as a vessel,

A simple boat for going here and there.

Make of it a wish-fulfilling gem

To bring about the benefit of beings.

THE WAY OF THE BODHISATTVA

When shall I depart to make my home

In cave or empty shrine or under spreading tree,

With, in my breast, a free, unfettered heart,

Which never turns to cast a backward glance?

THE WAY OF THE BODHISATTVA

The Buddha replied, "The greatest gain is to give to others;

the greatest loss is to receive without gratitude.

Patience is an invulnerable armor;

wisdom is the best weapon."

We are what we think.

All that we are arises with our thoughts.

With our thoughts we make the world.

Speak or act with a pure mind

And happiness will follow you

As your shadow, unshakable.

DHAMMAPADA

All things conditioned are instable, impermanent,

Fragile in essence, as an unbaked pot,

Like something borrowed, or a city founded on sand,

They last a short while only.

They are inevitably destroyed,

Like plaster washed off in the rains,

Like the sandy bank of a river—

They are conditioned, and their true nature is frail.

LALITAVISTARA

"All is transient." When one sees this, he is

above sorrow. This is the clear path.

DHAMMAPADA 20.277

From the world of the senses . . . comes heat and comes cold,

and pleasure and pain. They come and they go: they are transient.

Arise above them, strong soul.

The man whom these cannot move, whose soul is one,

beyond pleasure and pain, is worthy of life in Eternity.

One man dreams he lives a hundred years

Of happiness, but then he wakes.

Another dreams an instant's joy,

But then he, likewise, wakes.

And when they wake, the happiness of both

Is finished, never to return.

Likewise, when the hour of death comes round,

Our lives are over, whether brief or long.

THE WAY OF THE BODHISATTVA

[T]he Eternal in man cannot die.

He is never born, and he never dies.

He is in Eternity: he is for evermore.

BHAGAVAD GITA 2.19–20

He who in early days was unwise

but later found wisdom,

he sheds a light over the world

like that of the moon when free from clouds.

DHAMMAPADA 13.172

Who can trace the invisible path of the man who soars in the sky of

liberation, the infinite Void without beginning, whose passions are peace,

and over whom pleasures have no power?

His path is as difficult to trace as that of the birds in the air.

DHAMMAPADA 7.93

Look upon the man who tells thee thy faults as if he told thee of a

hidden treasure, the wise man who shows thee the dangers of life.

Follow that man: he who follows him will see good and not evil.

DHAMMAPADA 6.76

At the end of OM there is silence. It is a silence of joy.

It is the end of the journey where fear and sorrow are no more:

steady, motionless, never falling, ever-lasting, immortal.

MAITRI UPANISHAD

Do not pursue the past.

Do not lose yourself in the future.

The past no longer is.

The future has not yet come.

Looking deeply at life as it is

in the very here and now,

the practitioner dwells

in stability and freedom.

We must be diligent today.

To wait until tomorrow is too late.

Death comes unexpectedly.

How can we bargain with it?

BHADDEKARATTA SUTTA

May I be a guard for those who are protectorless,

A guide for those who journey on the road.

For those who wish to go across the water,

May I be a boat, a raft, a bridge.

THE WAY OF THE BODHISATTVA

Just as a man who has long been far away is welcomed with joy

on his safe return by his relatives, well-wishers and friends;

in the same way the good works of a man in his life

welcome him in another life,

with the joy of a friend meeting a friend on his return.

DHAMMAPADA 16.219–220

Few cross the river of time and are able to reach

Nirvana. . . . But those who . . . follow the path of

the law, they shall reach the other shore and go

beyond the realm of death.

DHAMMAPADA 6.85–86

Life is no different from nirvana,

Nirvana no different than life.

Life's horizons are nirvana's:

The two are exactly the same.

VERSES FROM THE CENTER

NAGARJUNA

IMPRESSIONS

It is shortly before dawn on my second morning in Nepal. I am in Sauraha, on the edge of Chitwan National Park. My home for the next few days is a modest collection of bungalows run by two Nepali brothers. The jungle is coming awake around me, one species at a time, like a symphony tuning up, and at the moment I can hear elephants nearby.

As I stumble out of my doorway, the younger of my proprietors approaches me, breathless. "Madame, Madame, there is a rhino by the river!" I grab my camera bag, he grabs my hand and we run, sloshing through the mud, jumping over narrow portions of the river until suddenly a hulking profile looms out of the fog, not thirty feet away. Eyes fastened on the rhinoceros, my companion nods toward a low-limbed tree, the closest refuge, and then raises a large rock to his shoulder. I focus my lens and with the sound of my shutter, the rhino turns slowly to face us. Neither of us dares breathe. But, upwind from us, the huge beast turns back and lumbers off in the opposite direction, as the thick mist closes in around him.

Early mornings that winter invariably found southern Nepal swaddled in a low enveloping mist. Men disappeared over bridges that led to nowhere. Women materialized in the forests from between the trees. Elephants and their mahouts would emerge from the dense gray-blue and then, in an instant, slip back in. It lent an aura of calm, quiet mystery to what was already exotic. By eight, the mist had burned off and the world as we expected it to be once more returned.

I started my Nepalese journey that year in the Terai, the flat subtropical portion of southern Nepal that dips into the Gangetic plain. Entering from India by bus to Sunauli, my first stop was Lumbini just to the west where, according to legend, Siddhartha Gautama—Buddha—was born in the Sacred Garden around 566 B.C. I paid homage and then moved on to Sauraha.

This was my second foray into Buddhist cultures, but by no means my last. Initially, I had gone out of curiosity, more to experience Buddhism than to study it. Throughout much of Asia, religion and spirituality are inextricably interwoven into the fabric of daily life. Buddhist cultures, infused with a philosophy based upon impermanence, compassion and absence of desire, felt softer, more tempered. The warmth and respectful optimism of its followers added a layer of serenity to the most mundane encounters. Prolonged exposure to such a soothing perspective proved both contagious and addictive. Ironically, the journeys themselves regularly tested my own sense of inner harmony, reminding me of the very fragile nature of human existence.

A few weeks later, I accepted an invitation to spend Christmas in Nepal's Manang Valley on the southern edge of the Tibetan plateau. Buddhism came to this region in the seventh century with the expansion of Tibet, and the Manang Valley and area directly beyond is home to a thriving Tibetan Buddhist community as well as to several medieval monasteries. Early on the morning of the twenty-third, three other passengers and I were directed to a small eight seater plane parked on the Pokara airstrip. While the ground crew replaced the front four seats of the plane with rolled up foam mattresses, cramming them in as tightly as possible, we joked about the odds of the cargo uncoiling and suffocating us in midair.

Once we were airborne, the landscape out our windows changed dramatically as we left the tropics behind. Our pilot flew north, threading his way around and beyond the Annapurna massif and although the plane appeared to keep a steady height above the ground, with the mountains rising steeply beside us, it felt as if we were diving into narrow valleys. As the canyons into which we flew deepened, the winds whistling through them intensified as well, buffeting our little plane from side to side. And we began to view the mattresses, and their potential for extra padding, not as the source of our demise but quite possibly as our salvation.

Abruptly, we rounded a corner and the terrain opened out to a large windswept bowl. A landing strip marked the center. Off to the left was a low brown hut with smoke curling from its chimney and a rickety fence propped against one side. Behind the fence stood five very padded figures, their brown leathery faces peering out toward the plane. The plane teetered down and stopped, and our feet touched solid ground to the muffled applause of mittens. Hoisting my pack, I headed vaguely northwest, down the only road in sight, feeling as if I were walking to the edge of the world. About an hour into my hike, a small man in a big fur hat and large turquoise earrings, his legs dangling low off either side of a squat shaggy pony, came hurtling down the road and then vanished in a cloud of dust. I did not see anyone else for hours.

Laid out before me was a moonscape of rocky cinnamon-colored desert, with Tilicho Peak rising to 7,134 meters at the valley's west end. The remaining peaks of the Annapurnas lay directly to my south. Mountain spires reaching up to a clear deep blue sky lined each side of the valley. Glaciers, with streams flowing off of them, stretched down toward the valley's base. And every hour or so, I would come upon a cluster of stone houses, prayer flags sprouting from their roofs, clinging to the cliff face.

Close to noon, a group of women wearing long gray wool chubas and carrying huge baskets on their backs, caught up with me and together we walked the last few paces to Manang. We crossed a stream, passed a small mill and headed uphill past a row of chortens, mani stones and, at the top, a series of prayer wheels, polished to a high sheen by thousands of turnings. Ducking under a low stone archway, we stepped onto a narrow shelf of land, crowded with houses piled one atop another. Far below, a glacial lake glistened aqua in the midday sun.

Later that afternoon, I located the elderly caretaker of the village gompa and persuaded her to unlock it. Stepping around a huge primary colored prayer wheel at the gompa doorway, we entered into a large open room lit only by a center skylight. As my eyes adjusted to the gloom, I could make out square cubbyholes housing Tibetan scripture all along one wall. From the other three, effigies, devils' masks and skulls grinned back at me in the dim light—eerie reminders of the Bon heritage of Tibetan Buddhism.

#　　#　　#　　#

The following summer, I had planned to go to Tibet. Periodic uprisings, however, had rendered the political situation uncertain. There were rumors of demonstrations in Lhasa and China seemed to be opening and closing the border on whim. Even from within China, the advice from the travelers' grapevine was simply to get as close as possible and just try. Wanting to see as much as I could, I opted to go overland, moving up from Hong Kong by combination of boat, bus and train through the ethnically Tibetan areas directly to Tibet's east and north, with the goal of ultimately traveling south from Golmud in Qinghai Province via the only route then legally available to foreigners. I stopped first at Lijiang, home to a distinctly matriarchal line of Tibetan descendants, and from there headed up to Chengdu, to Xiahe for a festival, and then on to Lanzhou, Xining and finally Golmud directly north of the Tibetan border.

My guidebook had warned that from Golmud to Hell was a local call. Upon arrival, I found that description exceedingly kind. The day was thickly overcast, without a hint of anything bright in the sky and dry, gray, dense clouds of sand, dust and probably potash from the nearby mine blew everywhere. The bus from the train station drove past endless drab apartment blocks and deposited me at the one hotel in town allowed to accept western travelers. I paid my fee and trudged up three flights of stairs to what the desk attendant had claimed was the sole available accommodation: a room of nineteen beds, eighteen of them occupied by languishing young westerners, most of them sick. There was one communal shower room for the entire four story hotel and it opened for women for one hour a day, between eight and nine in the evening when it was totally dark, both inside and out.

Despite an official timetable listing daily departures, buses transporting non-Chinese from Golmud to Lhasa were apparently infrequent and many travelers had been stranded for days. By the time I arrived, some of the younger ones were talking of storming the tourist office and demanding a bus, along the lines of a hijacking, or more aptly perhaps, a jail break. I was fortunate. There was a bus scheduled for the very next day and, unlike those for most of the days before, this one actually left.

The following morning, after several unexplained delays, a dilapidated bus, packed in with passengers, set off on a "luxury tour" to Lhasa: a punishing, thirty-eight hour, 1,115 kilometer allegedly nonstop ride south through some of the most breathtakingly beautiful terrain I have ever seen. As we jolted across the virtually uninhabited Tibetan plateau, the wild rugged beauty of the landscape unfolded before us. Crystalline light fell on miles of rolling dunes, making them glow at times, as if lit from below. Vast alpine meadows lay in the shadow of the Tanggula Shan, the snowcaps on the mountains repeating the shapes of nomads' tents at their base. Closer to Lhasa, the mountainside appeared to be draped in green or blue velvet.

Lhasa itself and, to a lesser extent, Tibet in general presented a jarring combination of ancient Tibetan spirituality and more recent Chinese occupation. But the fact that these two elements could coexist at all, however tenuously, stood as a testament to the strength and resilience of the Tibetan people. Despite the Chinese attempts at cultural genocide, pilgrims still thronged to Lhasa to circumambulate clockwise around the Barkhor, offer prayer scarves to the deities in the few rooms open in the Potala Palace, and prostrate themselves before the Jokhang, one of Tibet's holiest shrines. Although their ranks were a fraction of what they had once been, amidst raucous shouting and clapping, young monks debated the scriptures in monastery courtyards. The devout traveled to Tsurphu to pay their respects to the young Karmapa, a living Buddha, who bestowed his blessing by placing a small red thread—to be worn until it fell off—around the neck of each who filed in before him. They journeyed to the west to Mount Kailash, often prostrating the entire way. And once a year, before crowds of pilgrims, the monks unfurled giant silk thangkas on the hillsides behind their monasteries.

By the time of my visit, the Chinese had realized that even though Tibetan Buddhism was something they wanted to contain, it was also proving to be a huge source of tourist revenue, and thus was something they very much wanted to exploit. Consequently, the Chinese were beginning to permit refurbishment of many of the monasteries and temples that, during the Cultural Revolution, they had all but destroyed. Tucked away in the Yarlung Valley, the birthplace of Tibetan Buddhism, Samye, Tibet's first monastery, was undergoing massive restoration; forty kilometers east of Lhasa, Ganden monastery, one of the three traditional pillars of the Tibetan state, which had been completely destroyed by Chinese shelling, was also being rebuilt. Many of the buildings of Drepung monastery, however, just outside Lhasa, still lay in ruins. When I visited Drepung, the monks insisted that I photograph, "to show the world what the Chinese had done."

#   #   #   #

My return to the Himalayas was to Ladakh, via yet another bus trip, etched into my memory this time not merely for its scenic grandeur but also for the sheer terror it inspired. Ladakh, the "land of high mountain passes," lies between Pakistan and China in the northernmost region of India. Cradled between the Himalayas and the Karakorums, the two highest mountain ranges in the world, it is high altitude desert, well beyond the reach of the monsoons. Its capital, Leh, sits on a 3,500 meter high plateau in the middle of the Indus Valley, midway between the Punjab of India and Yarkhand in Central Asia. For centuries, Leh served as an important staging post for the southern route of the Silk Road. As a consequence, Ladakh became a major crossroads between Tibetan Buddhist culture from the east and Islamic influences from the west. Approximately eighty percent Buddhist, the area is home to two major Tibetan sects, the Gelukpa, headed by the Dalai Lama, and the Kagyu, who follow the teachings of Milarepa, an eleventh century tantric practitioner and poet. In Ladakh, I hoped to experience the culture without any political overlay.

Again, I chose to go by land and since trouble had flared up in Kashmir directly to the west, the eastern route from the

Indian hill station of Manali presented the only viable option. This road, however, had its own set of difficulties as it was never designed for the volume and weight of the traffic it was now required to support. Basically a one lane, largely unpaved jeep track, the Manali-Leh road snakes its way for 485 kilometers through an interminable series of switchbacks up and over the highest passes in the world. It came into service as a supply route for the Indian Army in the late 1980s and then, out of necessity, opened to western travelers in 1989. It has no guardrails and from the outside edge, which can give way at any time, sheer drops can plummet 500 meters or more. As the Kashmiri tensions had heightened, nearly all of the Ladakh traffic, primarily heavily laden supply trucks and buses, had been diverted to this eastern route. In the best of times, this road, the second highest motorable road in the world, is reputed to be the second most treacherous. By the time I reached it, monsoon rains in the southern half and freak snowstorms in its northern reaches had pelted the road with boulders and landslides, reducing it to a shifting dirt ledge.

I should have suspected that something was amiss when I went to the Manali ticket office to book my onward journey north. There was supposed to be a bus to Leh every day. But when I went in, the ticket agents gave me the option of either buying the last seat for the next morning's bus or waiting it out for another week. And they did seem overly concerned that I had enough food, water, blankets and necessary medication on the bus close to me, for the full duration of the trip. They stopped short, however, of explaining why.

As it turned out, my seat, on the outside, in the very last row, gave me a unique vantage point for the journey. Most of the time, I would look out the side window and see nothing but a straight drop down. Frequently, in the lower section between Manali and the Rohtang ("Piles of Dead Bodies") La, the first pass at 3,980 meters, the bus would lurch over huge gaps in the road. Too far in from the edge, I would just see air. Before we reached the watershed, I regularly heard and felt torrents of water pouring over the road. Glancing back, I would realize that we had just plowed through a boulder strewn waterfall, which was eating away at the road's diminishing outer shoulder.

All too often throughout the trip, I would feel the road crumble under the back tires as we passed over particularly weak spots. I learned to anticipate those areas as the driver would accelerate just before them. At the top of the highest passes, the bus engine would momentarily cut off, apparently from lack of oxygen, but the driver anticipated that as well. Somehow, we managed to pass descending trucks and buses. But, as we were going uphill, always we were on the outside. It became normal to look directly down and see, not the road beneath us but, depending on where we were, a sheer drop, a series of tightly wound switchbacks or, on some occasions, the buses or trucks that had not made the grade. Even hearing—and feeling—the road give way did not bother me after a while, most likely because once I felt it, I knew that we were almost clear.

What I never adjusted to, however, was sitting in the back, on the outside as our fully loaded bus, tilted backwards, did a K maneuver on the hairpin turns. During those times, I was never able to see any road at all from either the back or the side. Like a mantra, I would repeat to myself over and over, "The wheels are ahead, the wheels are ahead." In total, we traversed through twenty-seven hairpin turns in short succession to ascend the last 1,000 meters before crossing the Zanskar Range.

Toward the end of the first day of the trip, well after nightfall, our driver turned on the interior lights—making it difficult for us to see out—and accelerated, pushing the bus over the broken road just as fast as it could go. As the landscape careened wildly before our headlights, I remember thinking how much it resembled the simulated scenes from American disaster movies; the difference was that this was real.

When I could will myself to look, the scenery was spectacular. From the lush green forests and glens of the Himalayan foothills, we climbed up and over the main Himalayan ridge and then the Zanskar Range. After crossing the Zanskar Range at the 5,059 meter Lungalacha La, we entered into an area reminiscent of the badlands of the American West, although much more rugged and far grander in scale. Giant cathedral-like spires of rock glowed golden in the late afternoon sun, their columns of rock formation rising up in some spots directly from the road. We ascended through a series of gorges and over another pass to a broad plateau full of grazing sheep and goats. For most of the trip, apart from the widely spaced tea stops and the random Bihari road crew engaged in the Sisyphean task of repair, there had been no other hint of civilization. Here, crossing the Moray Plains, it was comforting not only to travel horizontally but also, with the sight of the livestock, to know that we must be near journey's end. Finally, after two long days, we reached the Tanglang La, the second highest motorable pass in the world. Its crest at 5,328 meters offered sweeping vistas of both the Karakorums and the Himalayas and sported an official Indian road sign proclaiming, "Unbelievable is it Not!"

Upon clearing the Tanglang La, our route dropped precipitously into the Indus Valley, an area of surreal, magical landscape. Tiny villages of traditional earthen and stone whitewashed Tibetan architecture began to dot the barren desert, their terraced fields adding dashes of green. We passed huge white chortens, mani walls and occasionally a gompa. Nearly to Leh, Tikse monastery, high up on a bluff, commanded a view of the entire valley. Dozens of white cubic monks' quarters and chortens formed a broad pyramid, stacked up against the hillside. At its pinnacle, the monastery—whitewashed on its lower floors, deep red and ocher on its upper stories and flanks—appeared more magnificent than the Potala Palace. Just past Tikse, roadside rock carvings of the five Buddhas of meditation, dating back to the eighth century, gazed out in welcome. In this pristine setting, surrounded by snowcapped peaks, it felt as if we had entered the last Shangri-la.

I found a room just above Leh with floor to ceiling windows on two full sides, allowing me to look out over barley fields and up to the mountains in one direction and across the old town to prayer flags and the abandoned royal palace in the other. Just beyond my guest house, a large prayer wheel with a bell sat over a stream and I would awaken those first few mornings to the sounds of children turning the wheel and ringing its bell on their way to school. Beautiful medieval gompas, most of them very much in use, were scattered throughout the Indus Valley, with the highest concentration within a few kilometers of Leh. Mornings, most held daily pujas, open to the public. Afternoons, you could often hear the little monks from inside the gompas belting out their lessons in unison. In nearby Spitok monastery, the monks were working on an intricate mandala made out of sand. When they finished, they put it on display for a few days and then, as a reminder of the transient nature of life, they took it to the river and destroyed it. Once I acclimatized, I set out to explore the outlying monasteries of Lamayuru (one of the oldest monasteries in Ladakh, believed to have sheltered Milarepa), Alchi (housing the finest surviving examples of Kashmiri style tenth and eleventh century Buddhist murals) and then Likkir.

Four of us sat wedged together in the back row of a minibus on the way to Likkir, our neck scarves pulled up and tucked under our sunglasses, covering our noses and mouths to save us from inhaling what felt like gallons of dust. At the first stop, a monk squeezed in among us, pulling his visor down low, grimacing sympathetically and then grinning before pulling his shawl up over his mouth as well. We bounced along listening to tinny Hindi music blaring from the speakers in the front, the starkness of the landscape out our windows interrupted only by startling thatches of low purple flowers. Well off the road, a solitary monk strode across the arid plain, spinning his prayer wheel, a dot of maroon against the expanse of ocher. Halfway there, the bus pulled over to pick up some villagers with their harvest. Everyone emptied out of the bus to help secure fragrant green bales onto the roof. We had not gone very far before the bus stopped again and everyone helped unload. Just after sunset, we arrived in Likkir.

Set high up in a narrow side valley, Likkir is home to one of the most important Gelukpa monasteries in Ladakh. Originally founded in 1065, the monastic community converted to Tibetan Buddhism in 1470; at the time of my visit, it was headed by the younger brother of the Dalai Lama. Located three kilometers up from the village, the monastery presides over a small oasis of stone houses and terraced fields, protected by steep mountain walls. It was harvest time when I was in Likkir and down below at the mouth of the valley, the villagers would sing as they brought in their yearly crop of barley. Farther up, the monks of Ladakh were consecrating a seventy-five meter high statue of the Maitreya (future) Buddha. For days, busfuls of maroon-robed monks wound their way up through the stretch of desert beyond the village to join in the celebration. Throughout those days, sounds of horns, conch shells, cymbals and drums, mixed with the low ritual intoning of Tibetan monks, drifted down through the valley, reverberating off the valley walls. As you moved up toward the monastery, away from the village, the sounds of the puja would gradually take over, until the cheerful voices of the villagers had faded completely.

At sunset, I would sit alone in the valley, above the fields but below the monastery, surrounded by the mountains, tinged with the last rays of the sun. A distant mountainside would brighten for a moment and then be darkened purple by a passing cloud. Rising up from the base of the valley, the harvesters' singing would meet the music and the chanting of the monks. The sounds floated around me, as the sun set and turned the burnished mountains to gold.

#   #   #   #

I spent months in the tropics as well working on the pictures for this book. There, the landscape was as lush as the mountains had been barren and often I felt immersed in a crush of humanity. Despite the physical differences, despite the harsh political situations in some of the areas I visited, the Buddhist cultures continued to instill a spirit of tranquility.

As in Tibet, the military junta which controlled Burma (Myanmar) regarded the Buddhist culture within its borders as a fertile source of tourist income—money that could then be channeled back into oppressing its people. Intent upon extracting as much foreign currency as possible, the Myanmar regime had instituted an extortionate system of foreign exchange, patterned after the one used in China, which gave its guests the equivalent of six cents on the dollar. To strengthen its grasp on our wallets and its control over our movements, the government also required that we use only officially sanctioned, and priced, accommodation and transport and that we record proof of our actions on a "money card" to be surrendered upon departure. The effect of this system was to drive even the most scrupulous of travelers to the black market for cash and, for most everything else, to the extensive underground network which had sprung up in the few years since Burma had cracked open its doors. For the outsider at least, the warmth and compassion of the Burmese people often counterbalanced, and frequently circumvented, the suffocating control and uniformly callous attitudes of their government and its representatives, making a journey in Burma one of extremes.

My first day in Yangon, discovering that the advice in my guidebook was woefully out of date and that I would quickly run through my money if I adhered to official rates (and, given the brutality the regime inflicted on its own citizens, apprehensive as to the consequences if I did not), I left a restaurant without ordering—tired, hungry and despondent. A few blocks away, I heard sandals slapping the pavement behind me, turned and saw the cook, still in his food-stained apron and undershirt, hurrying toward me. When he caught up with me, the cook made it very clear that he wanted me to come back to the restaurant with him. Touched by his concern, I did and when I had finished my meal, the owner refused to let me pay. I returned to the restaurant on my last day in Burma to thank them for their kindness and, by that point having become well acquainted with black market banking, to pay them for my dinner. But they claimed they didn't remember me and refused to accept any cash.

Bus crews regularly stashed my backpack well out of sight so that it would not be searched during the military road-blocks. Sometimes it went in with the spare gas tanks; more often, it was stowed in a trunk near the driver—the seat of choice for women and babies. This was a spontaneous action. I never asked them to do it and, in fact, was caught off guard the first time they did. And every city, it seemed, had a local contact willing to assist foreign travelers.

In Mandalay, my train arrived at four in the morning. I was the only passenger to disembark. Far down to my left, the Tourist Burma window—the place to which I should have gone directly—cast the sole square of light onto the darkened platform. From the rows of benches directly in front of me, a courtly middle-aged Burmese man—the man other travelers had suggested I find—rose from the shadows and, whispering, asked me where I wanted to go. I told him and, taking my pack, he led me away from the government's window, out of the station and onto a series of horse carts, minivans and jeeps that nine hours later let me off at Inle Lake. I paid the local price, a bonus for me, but I also paid the Burmese directly and avoided yet another contribution to the Myanmar regime.

I stayed as long as the Lao government would permit in Luang Prabang, the old imperial capital in the north. Nestled in the mountains, on a peninsula at the confluence of the Mekong and Khan Rivers, this small, well-preserved city is home to over thirty gilded wats, shrines and stupas and well over one hundred historic Lao-French buildings. Low mountains rise up beyond the far riverbank and vegetable fields ring the river's edge.

Each morning in Luang Prabang, I would join the townspeople on the street corner near my hotel as they and the local monks "made merit." Shortly before dawn, people would emerge from their houses carrying bamboo cylinders of hot rice or vegetables. The streets would otherwise be deserted and neighbors would quietly greet each other as they moved to their selected spots. As if on cue, long single file lines of saffron-robed monks, barely illuminated by the streetlights, would slowly come into focus, padding down the dusty street, the eldest in the lead, the lines sometimes meeting, crossing and moving on like dancers on a stage set. Silently, head bowed, eyes downcast, each monk would stop and pause as each of the townspeople placed a fingerful of food into his black lacquer begging bowl. Every morning, together, the citizenry and the monks reminded each other of the importance of both generosity and humility. Then each went about his day, as the early sunlight brought the first signs of traffic and commerce.

#   #   #   #

Several long trips to Asia yielded a kaleidoscope of images and memories. Some of them I managed to capture on film, others not. In the quiet of daybreak on a deserted beach in Thailand, two monks emerged backlit from a palm grove, glided past me and disappeared into the next cove. Farther out in the bay, a man walked across a low tide sandbar as if walking on water. In Mandalay, the beatific face of a young Buddhist nun, a traditional pink shawl over her shaved head, beamed out at me, perfectly framed in the back window of an overcrowded public bus. And on my last morning in Burma, as the sun rose over broad flat pastures, I looked out my train window and, in the first golden light, saw three women in vibrantly colored sarongs, baskets on their heads, gracefully swaying through the fields. Approaching them from the opposite direction was a long line of Buddhist monks. The sun's rays filtered between them. And each took his own path to the light.

Jackson Heights, New York
February 2003

157

ACKNOWLEDGMENTS

The author gratefully acknowledges permission to quote from the following works:

Advice to Rahula, Four Discourses of the Buddha, translated by Narada Thera and Bhikku Mahinda, Buddhist Publication Society (Kandy, Sri Lanka 1974).

An Anthology from the Samyutta Nikaya, translated by John D. Ireland, Buddhist Publication Society (Kandy, Sri Lanka 1981).

Being Good: Buddhist Ethics for Everyday Life, by Master Hsing Yun, translated by Tom Graham, Weatherhill, Inc. (New York 1998).

The Bhagavad Gita, translated by Juan Mascaro, Penguin Classics (London 1962). Copyright © Juan Mascaro 1962. Reproduced by permission of Penguin Books Ltd.

Buddhist Scriptures, selected and translated by Edward Conze, Penguin Classics (London 1959). Copyright © Edward Conze 1959. Reproduced by permission of Penguin Books Ltd.

The Buddhist Tradition, by William Theodore de Bary, copyright © 1969 by William Theodore de Bary. Used by permission of Modern Library, a division of Random House, Inc.

The Connected Discourses of the Buddha: A New Translation of the Samyutta Nikaya, © Bhikkhu Bodhi 2000. Reprinted with permission of Wisdom Publications, 199 Elm St., Somerville, MA 02144 U.S.A, www.wisdompubs.org.

The Dhammapada (The Path of Perfection), translated by Juan Mascaro, Penguin Classics (London 1973). Copyright © Juan Mascaro 1973. Reproduced by permission of Penguin Books Ltd.

The Dhammapada: The Sayings of the Buddha, by Thomas Byrom, copyright © 1976 by Thomas Byrom. Used by permission of Alfred A. Knopf, a division of Random House, Inc.

Flowers Fall, by Dogen, translated by Paul Jaffe. © 1996 by Paul Jaffe. Reprinted by arrangement with Shambhala Publications, Inc., Boston, www.shambhala.com.

hsin hsin ming: verses on the faith mind, by Sengtsan, translated by Richard B. Clark, White Pine Press (Buffalo, N.Y., 1984).

The Hundred Thousand Songs; selections from Milarepa, poet saint of Tibet, translated by Antoinette K. Gordon, Charles E. Tuttle Co. Inc. (Boston and Tokyo 1961).

The Illustrated Tibetan Book of the Dead: a new translation with commentary, by Stephen Hodge with Martin Boord, Godsfield Press (London 1999).

Looking Inward: Observations on the Art of Meditation, by K. Khao-suan-luang, translated by Thanissaro Bhikku, Metta Forest Monastery (Valley Center, CA, 1994).

Our Appointment with Life: Discourse on Living Happily in the Present Moment (1990) by Thich Nhat Hanh, reprinted with permission of Parallax Press, Berkeley, CA.

Sacred Books of the Buddhists, vol. 3, T. W. Rhys Davids, ed., Pali Text Society (Oxford 1977). Quoted by permission of the Pali Text Society, which owns the copyright in the work.

The Teachings of Buddha, compiled by Paul Carus, published by Rider. Reprinted by permission of The Random House Group Ltd.

The Teachings of the Compassionate Buddha, E. A. Burtt, ed., Mentor (New York 1991). Copyright © E. A. Burtt 1955, 1982.

The Udana: Inspired Utterances of the Buddha & The Itivuttaka: the Buddha's Sayings, translated by John D. Ireland, Buddhist Publication Society (Kandy, Sri Lanka 1997).

SOURCES

Ambalatthika Exhortation to Rahula (*Majjhima Nikaya No. 61*), p. 54, adapted from Narada Thera and Bhikku Mahinda, translators, *Advice to Rahula, Four Discourses of the Buddha* (Kandy, Sri Lanka: Buddhist Publication Society, 1974) at pp. 12–16.

Bhaddekaratta Sutta, p. 138, from Thich Nhat Hanh, *Our Appointment with Life: Discourse on Living Happily in the Present Moment* (Berkeley, Calif.: Parallax Press, 1990) at p. 5.

The Bhagavad Gita, pp. 2, 14, 56, 60, 66, 78, 114 and 124, from Juan Mascaro, translator, *The Bhagavad Gita* (London: Penguin Classics, 1962) at pp. 10, 11, 15, 23, 33, 41 and 85.

Brihadaranyaka Upanishad, p. 82, from Eknath Easwaran, translator, *The Upanishads* (Tomales, Calif.: Nilgiri Press, 1987) at p. 37.

Buddhacarita, p. 96, from Asvaghosa, *A Life of the Buddha, Sacred Books of the East, Volume XIX*, Samuel Beal, translator (Oxford: 1883), relied upon in Paul Carus, ed., *The Teachings of Buddha* (London: Rider, 1998) at p. 60 (originally published as *The Gospel of the Buddha* (Chicago: Open Court, 1915) and adapted in Jack Kornfeld, ed., *Teachings of the Buddha* (Boston: Shambhala Publications, Inc., 1996) at p. 123.

The Dhammapada, pp. 16, 24, 26, 46, 48, 50, 62, 70, 78, 112, 126, 128, 130, 144 and 146, from Juan Mascaro, translator, *The Dhammapada (The Path of Perfection)* (London: Penguin Classics, 1973) at pp. 39, 43, 44, 46, 47, 48, 49, 56, 60, 63, 67, 75, 76, 81 and 82.

The Dhammapada, pp. 80 and 108, from Thomas Byrom, *The Dhammapada: The Sayings of the Buddha* (New York: Alfred A. Knopf, 1976), as quoted in Thomas Byrom, *The Dhammapada: The Sayings of the Buddha* (Boston: Shambhala Pocket Classic, 1996) at pp. 1–2 and 36.

Hitopadesa, p. 68, from Juan Mascaro, translator, *The Dhammapada (The Path of Perfection)* (London: Penguin Classics, 1973) at pp. 27 and 30.

Katha Upanishad, p. 20, from Eknath Easwaran, translator, *The Upanishads* (Tomales, Calif.: Nilgiri Press, 1987) at p. 95.

Lalitavistara, p. 110, from William Theodore de Bary, ed., *The Buddhist Tradition* (New York: Vintage Books, 1972) at p. 96.

Looking Inward, p. 90, from K. Khao-suan-luang, *Looking Inward: Observations on the Art of Meditation*, Thanissaro Bhikku, translator (Valley Center, Calif.: Metta Forest Monastery, 1994).

Mahaparinibbana Sutta, p. 76, from T.W. Rhys Davids, ed., *Sacred Books of the Buddhists*, vol. 3 (Oxford: Pali Text Society, 1977) at p. 108.

Maitri Upanishad, pp. 36 and 132, from Juan Mascaro, translator, *The Dhammapada (The Path of Perfection)* (London: Penguin Classics, 1973) at pp. 28 and 29.

Samyutta Nikaya, p. 84, adapted from John D. Ireland, translator, *An Anthology from the Samyutta Nikaya* (Kandy, Sri Lanka: Buddhist Publication Society, 1981) XLVII.19.

Samyutta Nikaya, p. 38, adapted from Bhikkhu Bodhi, translator, *The Connected Discourses of the Buddha: A New Translation of the Samyutta Nikaya*, vol. 1 (Somerville Mass.: Wisdom Publications, 2000) at p. 158.

Shinran's Songs to Amida, p. 18, from E. A. Burtt, ed., *The Teachings of the Compassionate Buddha* (New York: Mentor, 1991) at p. 219.

Shobogenzo Genjokoan, p. 88, from Dogen, *Flowers Fall*, Paul Jaffe, translator (Boston: Shambhala Publications, Inc., 1996) at pp. 102-103.

The Story of the Rock Demoness of Ling-Ba, p. 52, from Antoinette

Gordon, translator, *The Hundred Thousand Songs: selections from Milarepa, poet saint of Tibet* (Boston: Charles E. Tuttle Co. Inc., 1961) at pp. 87–88.

Sutta Nipata, p. 44, from E. M. Hare, translator, *Woven Cadences of Early Buddhists* (London: Pali Text Society, 1944), quoted at pp. 79 and 82 of Edward Conze, ed., *Buddhist Scriptures* (London: Penguin Classics, 1959).

Taittiriya Upanishad, p. 86, from Eknath Easwaran, translator, *The Upanishads* (Tomales, Calif.: Nilgiri Press, 1987) at p. 138.

The Teachings of Buddha, p. 32, adapted from Paul Carus, *The Teachings of Buddha* (London: Rider, 1998) at p. 46.

The Teachings of Buddha, p. 106, from Paul Carus, *The Teachings of Buddha* (London: Rider, 1998) at p. 104 (relying upon Samuel Beal, *A catena of Buddhist scriptures from the Chinese* (London: Trubner, 1871)), as adapted in Jack Kornfeld, ed., *Teachings of the Buddha* (Boston: Shambhala Publications, Inc., 1996) at p. 86.

Tibetan Book of the Dead, pp. 6, 8, 10 and 12, adapted from W. Y. Evans-Wentz, translator, *The Tibetan Book of the Dead* (London: Oxford University Press, 1960) in *The Teachings of the Buddha*, Jack Kornfeld, ed. (Boston: Shambhala Publications, Inc., 1996) at p. 177.

Tibetan Book of the Dead, p. 22, from Stephen Hodge with Martin Boord, *The Illustrated Tibetan Book of the Dead: a new translation with commentary* (London: Godsfield Press, 1999) at p. 52.

Udana 6.2, p. 28, from John D. Ireland, translator, *The Udana: Inspired Utterances of the Buddha & The Itivuttaka: the Buddha's Sayings* (Kandy, Sri Lanka: Buddhist Publication Society, 1997).

Upanishads, p. 4, from Juan Mascaro, translator, *The Dhammapada (The Path of Perfection)* (London: Penguin Classics, 1973) introduction at p. 10.

Upasakashila Sutra, p. 58, from Master Hsing Yun, *Being Good: Buddhist Ethics for Everyday Life*, Tom Graham, translator (New York: Weatherhill, Inc., 1998) at pp. 91–92.

Verses from the Center, pp. 92, 94 and 148, from Nagarjuna, "Acts," "Awakening," "Change" and "Nirvana," (translations of *Mulamadhyamakakarika* 13, 17, 24 and 25) in Stephen Batchelor, *Verses from the Center* (New York: Riverhead Books, 2000) at pp. 103, 110–111, 124–125 and 129.

Verses on the Faith Mind, p. 40, from Sengtsan, *hsin hsin ming: verses on the faith mind*, Richard B. Clark, translator (Buffalo, N.Y.: White Pine Press, 1984).

The Way of the Bodhisattva, pp. 42, 64, 72, 74, 100, 102, 120 and 140, from Shantideva, *The Way of the Bodhisattva: a translation of the Bodhicharyavatara*, Padmakara Translation Group, translators (Boston: Shambhala Publications, Inc., 1997) at pp. 44, 51, 62, 66, 72, 86, 98 and 113.

PHOTOGRAPHS

Printed in Italy

First Edition

....

Manufacturing by Mondadori Printing, Verona

Book design by Sharon Collins and Eleen Cheung

Library of Congress Cataloging-in-Publication Data:

Collins, Sharon, 1952-

To the light: a journey through Buddhist Asia/ Sharon Collins.

 p. cm.

ISBN 0-393-05736-4

1. Buddhism—Asia, Southeastern—History. 2. Buddhism—China—Tibet—History. 3. Buddhism—Nepal—History. I. Title.

BQ408.C65 2003

294.3'095—dc21

2003046414

W. W. Norton & Company, 500 Fifth Avenue, New York, N. Y. 10110

www.wwnorton.com

W. W. Norton & Company Ltd., Castle House, 75/76 Wells Street, London W1T 3QT

1 2 3 4 5 6 7 8 9 0